HOW TO SELL RAPIDLY

AND WILDLY

Your Ultimate Guide To Mastering

Rapid And Wild Success in Business

JACK STEWART

Copyright

Disclaimer

The information provided in this book, "How to Sell Rapidly and Wildly," is intended for educational and informational purposes only. The author and publisher are not responsible for any actions taken by readers based on the content of this book.

The strategies and techniques discussed may not guarantee specific results, as success in sales can be influenced by various external factors. Readers are advised to exercise their own judgment and seek professional advice as needed before implementing any of the ideas presented in this book.

TABLE OF CONTENT

Introduction

In the vast realm of business, success is often seen as a distant horizon, shimmering with potential and promise. Every entrepreneur embarks on this journey with dreams of rapid growth and wild achievements, but only a select few manage to turn their aspirations into astonishing realities.

Welcome to **"HOW TO SELL RAPIDLY AND WILDLY: Your Ultimate Guide To Mastering Rapid And Wild Success in Business."** This isn't just another book about entrepreneurship; it's a transformative manual crafted to equip you with the precise strategies and insights that propel businesses from the realm of ordinary to the heights of extraordinary.

Imagine a scenario: a humble startup, driven by sheer determination and guided by the principles outlined in these pages, evolved into a global phenomenon in a remarkably short time. This is the story of Amara's Jewelry—a tale that serves as both an inspiration and a blueprint for the astonishing feats you can achieve with the right knowledge and approach.

Amara Knightley, an aspiring jewelry designer, began her journey with little more than a passion for her craft and a handful of handmade pieces. However, armed with the techniques you're about to discover, she transformed her passion into a thriving empire. Through strategic marketing, an unshakable mindset, and a deep understanding of her target audience, Amara's Jewelry rapidly captured the hearts of consumers around the world. The lessons from Amara's remarkable journey are woven into the fabric of this guide, providing you with actionable steps to replicate her wild success.

Whether you're a seasoned business owner aiming to rejuvenate your growth trajectory or an ambitious newcomer ready to take the entrepreneurial plunge, this guide is your compass to navigate the stormy seas of business with confidence and purpose. Each chapter is a treasure trove of insights, proven techniques, and real-world examples that illustrate the transformative power of mastering the art of rapid and wild success.

Prepare to embark on a journey that will challenge your perceptions, ignite your ambition, and equip you with the tools necessary to propel your business into the stratosphere of success. As you absorb the wisdom within these pages, remember that the difference between a good business and a legendary one lies in your ability to embrace change, innovate relentlessly, and execute fearlessly.

The path to rapid and wild success is before you—let's embark on this exhilarating journey together. Your dream of an extraordinary business is no longer just a

vision; it's the next chapter waiting to be
written.

Understanding the Need for Rapid and Wild Success

In a world that thrives on constant evolution and rapid change, the concept of success has undergone a remarkable transformation. No longer confined to the realm of steady and incremental growth, today's entrepreneurs are driven by a hunger for rapid and wild success. But what exactly does this mean, and why is it so crucial in the landscape of modern business?

Rapid and wild success isn't just about achieving growth at breakneck speed; it's about embracing a mindset that dares to shatter conventional boundaries. It's the audacious pursuit of extraordinary achievements that defy norms and propel businesses to unparalleled heights. This dynamic approach to success is not born out of impatience, but out of a keen understanding of the rapidly changing tides of the business world.

The need for rapid and wild success is driven by several factors:

- Market Dynamics: In today's hyper-connected world, markets can shift in the blink of an eye. New technologies, emerging trends, and changing consumer behaviors require businesses to adapt swiftly or risk becoming obsolete.
- Competitive Landscape: The global business arena is more competitive than ever before. To stand out and

capture market share, businesses must not only keep pace but surge ahead with innovations that disrupt the status quo.

- Consumer Expectations: Consumers now demand instant gratification, personalized experiences, and solutions that align seamlessly with their fast-paced lifestyles. Businesses that can't meet these expectations risk losing customers to those who can.
- Technology's Influence: Technological advancements have shortened the path to success. Leveraging automation, AI, and data analytics can accelerate growth and streamline processes like never before.
- Investor Appetite: Investors are increasingly drawn to ventures that

demonstrate the potential for rapid and substantial returns. A business poised for rapid and wild success is more likely to attract the attention and funding it needs to fuel its growth.

- Global Reach: The digital age has removed geographical barriers, allowing businesses to access markets around the world. Rapid success is no longer confined to local or regional domains; it can be achieved on a global scale.

To embark on the journey of rapid and wild success, entrepreneurs must embrace agility, innovation, and calculated risk-taking. This journey is not for the faint of heart—it requires a mindset that thrives on change, an unwavering commitment to excellence, and a willingness to challenge the status quo.

As we delve deeper into this guide, each subsequent chapter will equip you with the tools, strategies, and insights needed to navigate the exhilarating yet unpredictable terrain of rapid and wild success. From unleashing innovation to mastering strategic marketing, you'll discover how to harness the winds of change and set sail on a transformative voyage towards unprecedented achievement. So, ready yourself to push boundaries, rewrite rules, and redefine your notion of success—because the journey starts now.

Setting the Stage for Business Growth

Before the crescendo of rapid and wild success can be heard, the stage must be meticulously set. Just as a conductor orchestrates each note before a symphony, entrepreneurs must lay the foundation for growth with precision and foresight. This phase is where dreams are translated into actionable plans, and aspirations take their first steps towards becoming reality.

1. Crafting a Clear Vision: Every remarkable journey begins with a clear destination in mind. Define your business's purpose, mission, and values. This vision will serve as a guiding light, helping you stay focused and

aligned as you navigate the turbulent waters of growth.

2. Strategic Planning: Map out a strategic plan that outlines your business goals, target markets, and competitive landscape. Identify the challenges and opportunities that lie ahead and chart a course to steer your business towards success.

3. Building a Solid Foundation: Just as a skyscraper requires a robust foundation, your business needs strong fundamentals. Establish efficient operational processes, a scalable organizational structure, and a supportive company culture that fosters innovation and collaboration.

4. Financial Preparedness: Adequate financial resources are the lifeblood of growth. Assess your capital needs and secure funding sources to fuel expansion, whether through investments, loans, or internal cash flow.

5. Market Research: Gain a deep understanding of your target audience, their needs, and preferences. Use market research to uncover unmet demands and areas where your business can excel.

6. Product/Service Refinement: Before the spotlight shines brightly, ensure your offerings are finely tuned. Continuously refine and innovate your products or services to meet the evolving expectations of your customers.

7. Branding and Identity: Craft a compelling brand identity that resonates with your audience. Your brand should convey your unique value proposition and set you apart from competitors in the marketplace.

8. Customer Engagement Strategy: In a world brimming with choices, customer loyalty is the golden ticket to success. Develop a strategy for engaging and retaining customers through exceptional service, personalized experiences, and continuous communication.

9. Technology Integration: Embrace technology as an enabler of growth. Identify tools and systems that streamline processes, enhance customer experiences, and provide

data-driven insights for strategic decision-making.

10. Legal and Regulatory Compliance: As you set the stage, ensure that your business adheres to all relevant legal and regulatory requirements. This will protect your venture from potential setbacks and legal disputes.

Setting the stage for business growth is a deliberate and calculated endeavor. It's a time of preparation, of fine-tuning the instruments, and of laying the groundwork for the symphony of success that's about to unfold. With each piece in place, you're poised to embark on the exhilarating journey towards rapid and wild success. As you step onto this stage, remember that every note you play, every decision you

make, and every strategy you implement
will shape the melody of your business's
growth story. The spotlight awaits—let the
performance begin.

Developing a Winning Mindset

In the high-stakes arena of business, a winning mindset is the X-factor that distinguishes the ordinary from the extraordinary. It's the foundation upon which rapid and wild success is built—a reservoir of resilience, innovation, and unwavering determination. Just as a captain steers a ship through treacherous waters, entrepreneurs navigate the complexities of business with a mindset that can weather storms and seize opportunities.

1. Embrace Change as an Ally: In a world of constant flux, change is inevitable. A winning mindset embraces change not as a

threat, but as an ally. It sees disruption as an opportunity to innovate, adapt, and gain a competitive edge.

2. Cultivate Resilience: Setbacks and challenges are part and parcel of the entrepreneurial journey. A winning mindset thrives in adversity, using failures as stepping stones and setbacks as fuel for growth.

3. Learn from Experience: Every success and failure holds valuable lessons. A winning mindset views experiences as a wellspring of wisdom, learning from mistakes and using triumphs as blueprints for future victories.

4. Pursue Lifelong Learning: The pursuit of knowledge is unceasing. A winning mindset hungers for continuous learning, staying updated on industry trends, emerging technologies, and evolving customer preferences.

5. Embrace Risk-Taking: Calculated risks are the gateway to innovation and growth. A winning mindset encourages calculated risk-taking, understanding that rewards often lie just beyond the borders of the comfort zone.

6. Think Big and Bold: A winning mindset defies limitations. It dares to think big and envisage grand possibilities. It's the wellspring of audacious goals and the fuel

that propels entrepreneurs beyond the boundaries of conventional thinking.

7. Maintain a Positive Attitude: Positivity is the backbone of success. A winning mindset radiates positivity, fostering a can-do attitude that influences teams, attracts opportunities, and propels businesses forward.

8. Focus on Solutions: Challenges are merely puzzles waiting to be solved. A winning mindset shifts focus from problems to solutions, seeking innovative approaches and collaborating to overcome obstacles.

9. Adapt to New Realities: The business landscape evolves rapidly. A winning mindset remains adaptable, ready to pivot,

and agile enough to seize new opportunities as they emerge.

10. Surround Yourself with Positivity: The company you keep influences your mindset. A winning mindset seeks out mentors, peers, and partners who share its positivity, drive, and ambition.

11. Visualize Success: Visualization is a powerful tool. A winning mindset paints a vivid picture of success, empowering you to stay focused, motivated, and aligned with your goals.

12. Celebrate Achievements: Every step forward is a victory worth celebrating. A winning mindset recognizes achievements,

no matter how small, and uses them as fuel for sustained momentum.

Developing a winning mindset is the keystone of your journey towards rapid and wild success. It's the compass that guides your decisions, the armor that shields you from doubt, and the fire that propels you towards your dreams. As you embark on this transformational voyage, remember that your mindset is the sculptor of your reality—it has the power to shape challenges into opportunities and aspirations into accomplishments. With a winning mindset, you're not just an entrepreneur; you're a force to be reckoned with.

Cultivating a Growth-Oriented Perspective

In the fertile soil of entrepreneurship, a growth-oriented perspective is the seed from which monumental success blossoms. It's the mindset that propels individuals and businesses beyond their current limitations, unlocking uncharted territories of achievement. Just as a gardener tends to their plants with care, entrepreneurs nurture a growth-oriented perspective to foster innovation, resilience, and boundless potential.

1. Embrace the Power of Possibility: A growth-oriented perspective sees every challenge as an opportunity. Instead of

fixating on limitations, it focuses on the potential for growth and advancement.

2. Relish in Continuous Improvement: The journey of growth is a marathon, not a sprint. A growth-oriented perspective revels in incremental progress, understanding that even small steps can accumulate into significant achievements.

3. Learn from Feedback: Feedback is a compass pointing towards improvement. A growth-oriented perspective welcomes constructive criticism and treats failures as stepping stones towards mastery.

4. Embody a Curious Mind: Curiosity fuels exploration and innovation. A growth-oriented perspective approaches

situations with an open mind, eager to learn, explore, and adapt.

5. Shift from Competition to Collaboration: Instead of viewing others as competition, a growth-oriented perspective sees potential collaborators and sources of inspiration. It thrives on sharing knowledge and collaborating to create win-win situations.

6. Challenge Comfort Zones: Growth lies just beyond the edges of comfort zones. A growth-oriented perspective actively seeks out challenges and novel experiences, recognizing that this is where true expansion occurs.

7. Set Goals with Purpose: Goals are the compass that guides growth. A

growth-oriented perspective sets clear, meaningful goals that provide direction and purpose for every endeavor.

8. Embrace Failure as a Teacher: Failures are integral to growth. A growth-oriented perspective reframes failures as valuable lessons, allowing setbacks to fuel determination and resilience.

9. Nurture a "Yet" Mentality: Instead of saying "I can't," adopt a "I can't yet" attitude. A growth-oriented perspective recognizes that skills and abilities can be developed over time with effort and practice.

10. Cultivate a Long-Term View: Immediate gratification may be tempting, but a

growth-oriented perspective understands the value of delayed rewards. It prioritizes long-term gains over short-term fixes.

11. Reflect and Adapt: Periodic reflection fuels growth. A growth-oriented perspective takes time to evaluate progress, adjust strategies, and make informed decisions for ongoing development.

12. Celebrate Milestones: Celebrating milestones is a reminder of progress. A growth-oriented perspective takes the time to acknowledge achievements, no matter how small, as they contribute to the bigger picture.

Cultivating a growth-oriented perspective is the cornerstone of your evolution as an entrepreneur. It's the mindset that turns challenges into stepping stones and setbacks into opportunities. With this perspective as your guiding star, you're poised to not only weather the storms of business but to harness their energy to drive your journey of continuous expansion. Remember, growth is not just a destination; it's a perpetual journey of self-improvement, innovation, and reaching ever higher towards your potential.

Overcoming Fear and Embracing Risk

Fear and risk are the twin gatekeepers that stand between entrepreneurs and the realm of extraordinary success. They cast a shadow of doubt, discouraging many from venturing beyond their comfort zones. Yet, it is precisely at the intersection of fear and risk that growth flourishes, innovations thrive, and the extraordinary becomes attainable. To truly master the art of rapid and wild success, one must learn to silence the echoes of fear and dance with the unknown.

1. Understand the Nature of Fear: Fear is a primal response designed to keep us safe. Acknowledge it, but don't let it paralyze you.

Instead of resisting fear, learn to harness its energy and transform it into courage.

2. Reframe Failure: Failure is a vital component of growth. Embrace it as a stepping stone towards success, viewing each setback as a lesson that brings you one step closer to your goals.

3. Calculate Risks: While embracing risk is essential, it's equally important to assess risks intelligently. Evaluate potential outcomes, weigh pros and cons, and make informed decisions.

4. Break Down the Unknown: The unknown can be intimidating, but breaking it down into smaller, manageable steps makes it less daunting. Take one step at a time, and each

small victory will empower you to face bigger challenges.

5. Set Realistic Expectations: Embrace the possibility of failure, but also the potential for great success. Setting realistic expectations helps you manage your fears and focus on the journey rather than the outcome.

6. Cultivate a Growth Mindset: A growth mindset sees challenges as opportunities to learn and grow. Embrace challenges as chances to develop new skills and expand your capabilities.

7. Visualize Success: Visualization can help quell fear. Imagine the positive outcomes of

taking risks, and let those images guide you through moments of uncertainty.

8. Seek Support: Surround yourself with a supportive network of mentors, peers, and friends who can provide guidance and encouragement when facing risks.

9. Embrace Discomfort: Growth happens outside of comfort zones. Embrace discomfort as a sign that you're pushing boundaries and inching closer to your goals.

10. Celebrate Courage: Acknowledge and celebrate instances where you've overcome fear and taken calculated risks. These small victories build your resilience and bolster your confidence.

11. Focus on Growth, Not Perfection: Shift your focus from achieving perfection to achieving growth. Accept that mistakes will happen, and they'll be valuable stepping stones on your journey.

12. Reflect on Regrets: Imagine looking back and regretting not taking a chance. Let this perspective motivate you to embrace risks now, rather than wondering "what if" later.

To sell rapidly and wildly, you must be willing to embrace the unfamiliar, to step onto uncharted terrain, and to confront your fears head-on. Remember, it's not about eliminating fear; it's about harnessing its energy to propel you forward. As you embrace risk, you're not just navigating the unknown; you're sculpting the contours of your success story, one daring decision at a time. Each calculated risk is a brushstroke on the canvas of your journey, creating a masterpiece of innovation, growth, and unbridled achievement.

Identifying Lucrative Opportunities

In the bustling landscape of business, opportunities are the hidden gems that hold the promise of prosperity. However, not all opportunities are created equal, and the ability to identify the most promising ones is a skill that separates successful entrepreneurs from the rest. Like a skilled prospector, you must navigate the terrain of possibilities with a discerning eye and a strategic mindset to uncover the gold mines of potential that lie beneath the surface.

1. Stay Attuned to Trends: Keep a finger on the pulse of industry trends, technological advancements, and shifts in consumer

behavior. Opportunities often arise where demand meets innovation.

2. Address Unmet Needs: Identifying gaps in the market is a surefire way to uncover lucrative opportunities. Look for areas where customer needs are underserved or overlooked.

3. Analyze Market Data: Utilize market research and data analysis to identify niches, emerging markets, and underserved segments that could be your ticket to success.

4. Observe Competitive Landscapes: Study your competitors to find gaps they might be leaving in the market. Look for areas where

you can provide better value or a unique selling proposition.

5. Leverage Your Expertise: Your unique skills and knowledge can lead you to untapped opportunities. Identify areas where your expertise can fill a void or provide a competitive advantage.

6. Follow Innovations: Keep an eye on emerging technologies and innovations. Opportunities often arise where existing industries intersect with cutting-edge advancements.

7. Listen to Customers: Pay attention to customer feedback and pain points. These insights can guide you toward opportunities for creating solutions that resonate.

8. Collaborate and Network: Collaborations and partnerships can open doors to new opportunities. Networking with other professionals can lead to unexpected avenues for growth.

9. Evaluate Economic Shifts: Economic changes can create new opportunities. Anticipate shifts in the market that might open doors for your business.

10. Explore Global Markets: Expanding beyond your local market can uncover fresh opportunities. Research international markets to find areas where your offerings could thrive.

11. Test and Experiment: Experiment with new ideas on a small scale before fully committing. This allows you to test the waters and assess the potential of an opportunity.

12. Adapt and Pivot: Be open to adapting your initial plans based on market feedback and changing circumstances. This flexibility can help you seize unforeseen opportunities.

Identifying lucrative opportunities is a blend of insight, research, and a touch of intuition. It's the art of spotting potential where others see routine. As you delve into this pursuit, remember that each opportunity is a puzzle piece in the larger picture of your business's success. With each discovery, you're not just uncovering potential for growth; you're forging a path toward the rapid and wild success that awaits those who dare to explore and seize the unknown.

Market Research and Trend Analysis

In the ever-evolving landscape of business, market research and trend analysis are the compasses that guide entrepreneurs through uncharted territory. They provide the insights needed to navigate the shifting currents of consumer preferences, technological advancements, and competitive forces. Just as an explorer charts a course with meticulous detail, entrepreneurs rely on market research and trend analysis to unveil opportunities, mitigate risks, and make informed decisions that propel them toward rapid and wild success.

1. Understand Consumer Behavior: Market research delves deep into consumer behavior, uncovering preferences, buying habits, and pain points. This knowledge allows you to tailor your offerings to precisely meet their needs.

2. Identify Emerging Trends: Trend analysis identifies patterns and shifts in the market landscape. By staying ahead of emerging trends, you can position your business to seize opportunities before they become mainstream.

3. Evaluate Competition: Researching competitors helps you understand your strengths and weaknesses relative to others in the market. This knowledge informs your strategy and differentiates your offerings.

4. Gauge Market Size and Demand: Quantify the potential of your market by assessing its size and the demand for your product or service. This information aids in setting realistic goals and expectations.

5. Test Product/Market Fit: Market research helps validate your product or service's fit within the market. It provides insights into whether your offering addresses a genuine need or solves a problem.

6. Analyze Customer Feedback: Feedback from customers is a treasure trove of insights. Listen to their suggestions, complaints, and compliments to fine-tune your offerings.

7. Stay Ahead of Competitors: Trend analysis enables you to anticipate competitive moves and prepare strategic responses. Staying ahead of the curve is a key driver of rapid success.

8. Innovate with Data: Data-driven insights guide innovation. By analyzing market trends and consumer behavior, you can identify gaps to fill and creative ways to improve.

9. Tailor Marketing Strategies: Understanding your audience's preferences allows you to create targeted marketing campaigns that resonate with potential customers.

10. Forecast Future Demand: By studying historical data and emerging trends, you can make educated predictions about future market demand.

11. Reduce Risks: Informed decisions are inherently less risky. Market research and trend analysis help you minimize potential pitfalls by basing decisions on evidence.

12. Pivot with Precision: When circumstances change, the ability to pivot becomes essential. A thorough understanding of market trends helps you pivot in a direction that aligns with evolving demands.

Market research and trend analysis aren't just tools; they're the foundation upon which informed strategies are built. As you embark on the journey to rapid and wild success, remember that these insights are the wind in your sails, propelling you forward with confidence. The data you gather and the trends you decipher aren't mere statistics; they're the keys that unlock doors to innovation, customer satisfaction, and unparalleled achievement. With each informed decision, you're not just navigating the market; you're steering your business toward the apex of success.

Recognizing Unmet Needs and Niche Markets

In the vast tapestry of business opportunities, unmet needs and niche markets are the threads that weave innovation and success. While the mainstream market caters to broad demands, hidden within the fabric are pockets of untapped potential—gaps waiting to be filled and specific segments yearning for tailored solutions. Entrepreneurs who possess the acumen to recognize these uncharted territories of opportunity are poised to carve their own unique path to rapid and wild success.

1. Listen to the Whispers: Pay attention to the whispers of dissatisfaction among

consumers. These soft murmurs often hint at unmet needs and untapped niches.

2. Identify Pain Points: Unmet needs often manifest as persistent pain points. Identify challenges that are prevalent but lack adequate solutions.

3. Observe Behaviors: Watch how consumers interact with existing products and services. Their behaviors can reveal areas where improvements are needed.

4. Analyze Gaps: Niche markets are often born from gaps in the market. Analyze industries, products, or services to uncover areas where demand is underserved.

5. Leverage Your Expertise: Your unique skills and background can lead you to unexplored niches. Your knowledge can translate into solutions that others might overlook.

6. Follow Passionate Communities: Communities of passionate enthusiasts often point to niche markets. These groups have specific needs that may not be addressed by mass-market offerings.

7. Be Open to Cross-Industry Insights: Insights from one industry can be applied to another. Look for innovative ways to bridge gaps between industries.

8. Study Demographics: Demographic shifts and changes can create new opportunities.

Identify demographic groups that are growing or changing and consider their unique needs.

9. Innovate for the Future: Anticipate future needs by analyzing emerging technologies, social trends, and changing consumer behaviors.

10. Solve Problems Creatively: Think beyond conventional solutions. Innovative problem-solving can uncover niche markets that haven't been explored.

11. Test and Refine: Once you identify a potential niche, test your ideas and refine your offerings based on real-world feedback.

12. Build Relationships: Niche markets often thrive on strong relationships. Engage with your target audience to understand their needs and tailor your offerings accordingly.

Recognizing unmet needs and niche markets requires a blend of empathy, creativity, and strategic thinking. It's about spotting the spaces where your skills intersect with demand and creating solutions that resonate deeply with a specific audience. As you embark on this journey, remember that these uncharted territories hold not only potential profits but also the satisfaction of making a meaningful impact. Each unmet need you address and each niche you serve is a testament to your ability to perceive opportunities where others see only voids. With each innovative solution, you're not just fulfilling a need; you're shaping the landscape of your business's success.

Creating a Compelling Value Proposition

In the bustling marketplace where choices abound, a compelling value proposition is the beacon that guides customers to your doorstep. It's the powerful message that communicates not only what you offer but also why it matters. Like an artist crafting a masterpiece, entrepreneurs must skillfully weave together the threads of innovation, differentiation, and customer-centricity to create a value proposition that resonates deeply and sets their business apart.

1. Understand Your Audience: Before crafting a value proposition, you must intimately understand your target

audience—their desires, pain points, and aspirations.

2. Identify Unique Benefits: What sets your offering apart from the competition? Identify the unique benefits that only your product or service can provide.

3. Solve a Problem: A compelling value proposition addresses a specific problem or need your audience faces. Clearly articulate how your offering provides a solution.

4. Focus on Customer Outcomes: Instead of just listing features, highlight the outcomes your customers can achieve by using your product or service.

5. Offer Clear Differentiation: Articulate what makes you different from the rest. Whether it's quality, innovation, price, or service, your differentiation is key.

6. Keep It Clear and Concise: Your value proposition should be succinct and easy to understand. Aim for clarity that resonates even in a glance.

7. Use Strong Language: Choose impactful words that evoke emotion and excitement. Your language should convey confidence in the value you offer.

8. Highlight Tangible Results: If possible, quantify the benefits your customers can expect. Numbers and data add credibility and make your proposition more concrete.

9. Test and Refine: Experiment with different versions of your value proposition and gather feedback. Refine it based on what resonates best with your audience.

10. Align with Brand Identity: Your value proposition should align with your brand's identity and messaging. It should feel authentic and consistent.

11. Address Objections: Anticipate potential objections and address them in your value proposition. This builds trust and reassures customers.

12. Evolve with Your Audience: As your audience evolves, so should your value proposition. Continuously assess their

changing needs and update your messaging accordingly.

A compelling value proposition isn't just a tagline; it's the heart and soul of your business's identity. It's the promise you make to your customers and the foundation upon which loyalty is built. Crafting a value proposition that truly resonates requires a deep understanding of your audience, a keen awareness of your strengths, and an unwavering commitment to delivering on your promises.

As you craft your value proposition, remember that you're not just selling a product or service; you're selling a transformation, an experience, and a promise of value that enriches the lives of your customers. With each word you choose, you're sculpting the narrative of your business's essence, drawing customers in and igniting their curiosity.

Crafting Your Unique Selling Proposition (USP)

In the symphony of business, your Unique Selling Proposition (USP) is the distinct melody that captures attention, resonates with customers, and sets your brand apart in a sea of choices. It's the harmony of innovation, value, and relevance that strikes a chord with your audience. Just as a composer weaves together notes to create an unforgettable melody, entrepreneurs must craft a USP that harmonizes the essence of their offering with the needs of their customers.

1. Identify Your Unique Angle: Pinpoint what makes your offering truly unique. It

could be a feature, a benefit, a process, or a combination thereof.

2. Solve a Specific Problem: A powerful USP addresses a specific pain point or need your audience has, offering a solution that's unlike any other.

3. Highlight Key Benefits: Clearly articulate the benefits customers gain from choosing your product or service. Focus on what sets you apart and why it matters.

4. Be Clear and Concise: Your USP should be easy to understand and communicate in a sentence or two. Clarity is key in capturing attention.

5. Make an Emotional Connection: Weave emotional appeal into your USP. It should evoke feelings that resonate with your target audience.

6. Focus on Value: Showcase the value your customers receive. Whether it's cost savings, time efficiency, or an unmatched experience, emphasize why it matters.

7. Test and Iterate: Experiment with different versions of your USP and gather feedback. Continuously refine it based on what resonates most with your audience.

8. Convey Credibility: If possible, back up your USP with evidence, testimonials, or statistics that showcase your claim's validity.

9. Be Consistent: Ensure your USP aligns with your brand identity and remains consistent across all touchpoints, from marketing materials to customer interactions.

10. Address Pain Points: If your USP specifically addresses a common pain point in your industry, you're more likely to capture the attention of your target audience.

11. Think Long-Term: Your USP should have longevity. Avoid focusing solely on fleeting trends and aim for a proposition that remains relevant over time.

12. Adapt and Evolve: As your business evolves and your market changes, be

prepared to adjust your USP to maintain its effectiveness.

Crafting a compelling USP isn't just about finding the right words; it's about encapsulating the essence of your brand in a way that resonates with your audience. Your USP should be a promise of value, a declaration of what sets you apart, and a reflection of the impact you aim to make.

As you craft your USP, remember that you're not just creating a tagline; you're crafting a promise that will guide your business's identity, influence customers' decisions, and leave an indelible mark on the minds of those you serve. With each word you choose, you're composing a narrative that invites customers to become part of your story and to experience the unique symphony only your brand can provide.

Communicating Value to Your Target Audience

In the bustling marketplace, the ability to effectively communicate the value of your offerings to your target audience is the key that unlocks the doors of customer engagement and loyalty. It's the bridge that connects your brand's promise with the needs and aspirations of your customers. Just as a skilled storyteller weaves a tale that captivates and resonates, entrepreneurs must craft a narrative that speaks directly to their audience, conveying the impact, benefits, and relevance of what they offer.

1. Understand Your Audience: Begin by deeply understanding your target audience—their desires, pain points, and

preferences. Tailor your messaging to resonate with their specific needs.

2. Focus on Solutions: Highlight the problems your product or service solves. Showcase how you provide solutions that make your customers' lives better or easier.

3. Emphasize Benefits: Instead of just listing features, focus on the benefits customers gain from using your offering. Explain how it improves their lives or addresses their concerns.

4. Tell a Story: Craft a narrative that tells the story of your brand and its journey. Make it relatable, engaging, and aligned with the values of your audience.

5. Use Clear Language: Avoid jargon and complex terms. Use simple, clear language that is easily understood by your target audience.

6. Address Objections: Anticipate potential objections and address them in your communication. This builds trust and reassures customers.

7. Utilize Visuals: Visual elements can enhance your message's impact. Use images, videos, and infographics to convey your value proposition effectively.

8. Highlight Social Proof: Showcase testimonials, reviews, case studies, or endorsements from satisfied customers to add credibility to your claims.

9. Personalize Messages: Tailor your communication to resonate with different segments of your audience. A personalized approach shows you understand their unique needs.

10. Be Authentic: Authenticity builds trust. Be honest about what you offer, and avoid making exaggerated claims.

11. Address the "Why": Explain not only what you offer, but why it matters. Help your audience understand the impact your product or service can have on their lives.

12. Use Emotional Appeal: Emotions drive decisions. Craft messages that evoke feelings

your audience can connect with, such as joy, relief, or aspiration.

Effectively communicating value requires a delicate balance of empathy, storytelling, and strategic messaging. Your goal is to create a narrative that resonates deeply with your audience, drawing them into a journey that promises transformation and fulfillment. As you communicate value, remember that you're not just delivering information; you're fostering a connection, building trust, and inviting your audience to become an integral part of your brand's story. With each message you craft, you're not just relaying facts; you're painting a vivid picture of the positive impact your offering can have, sparking curiosity and

igniting the desire to experience that value
firsthand.

Building a Stellar Product or Service

In the realm of business, a stellar product or service is the North Star that guides customers toward your brand, keeps them engaged, and compels them to return. It's the embodiment of quality, innovation, and customer-centricity that sets your business apart and drives success. Just as a craftsman meticulously shapes each piece of a masterpiece, entrepreneurs must pour their expertise, dedication, and creativity into creating offerings that not only meet needs but exceed expectations.

1. Start with Customer Needs: Begin by understanding the specific needs and pain points of your target audience. Your product

or service should be designed to address these challenges effectively.

2. Focus on Quality: Quality is non-negotiable. Every aspect of your offering, from materials to design, should reflect your commitment to excellence.

3. Innovate for Improvement: Continuously seek ways to innovate and improve your offering. Whether it's through new features, technology, or design, innovation keeps your brand fresh and relevant.

4. Simplicity and User-Friendliness: Keep your product or service user-friendly and intuitive. Complexity can deter customers, while simplicity enhances the user experience.

5. Deliver on Promises: Whatever value proposition you communicate, make sure your product or service lives up to it. Consistency builds trust.

6. Personalization: Tailor your offering to meet individual customer needs as much as possible. Personalization enhances the sense of value and relevance.

7. Test and Refine: Before launch, test your product or service rigorously to identify and rectify any issues. Gather feedback and make improvements based on real-world use.

8. Prioritize Customer Experience: The customer journey matters. From the first

interaction to post-purchase support, prioritize a seamless and positive experience.

9. Incorporate Feedback: Listen to customer feedback and use it to enhance your offering. This not only improves the product but also shows customers that their opinions matter.

10. Adapt to Changes: Be prepared to adapt your product or service based on changing market trends, customer preferences, and technological advancements.

11. Sustainable Practices: Incorporate sustainable practices into your offering, if possible. Today's consumers value

environmentally responsible products and services.

12. Stand for Value: Your product or service should align with your brand's values and mission. This authenticity resonates with customers who share similar values.

Building a stellar product or service is a labor of love, requiring meticulous attention to detail, a passion for excellence, and a deep understanding of your audience. Your offering should be more than just functional; it should evoke emotions, solve problems, and leave a lasting impression. As you pour your creativity and expertise into crafting your offering, remember that you're not just creating a product or service; you're creating an experience, a solution, and a reflection of your dedication to making a positive impact. With each design choice, feature enhancement, and customer interaction, you're not just building a product or service; you're crafting an embodiment of value that resonates with your customers and stands as a testament to your commitment to excellence.

Designing for Quality and Innovation

In the realm of business, designing for quality and innovation is the blueprint for creating offerings that stand the test of time and captivate the imagination of your audience. It's the fusion of craftsmanship and forward-thinking that elevates your brand above the ordinary and into the realm of the extraordinary. Just as an architect meticulously plans each detail of a masterpiece, entrepreneurs must infuse their products or services with a commitment to excellence and a spirit of innovation that inspires awe and admiration.

1. Start with Purpose: Clearly define the purpose of your offering. What problem does it solve? How does it enhance lives? A purpose-driven approach ensures alignment with customer needs.

2. User-Centric Design: Place the user at the center of your design process. Consider their needs, preferences, and pain points to create an intuitive and satisfying experience.

3. Prioritize Functionality: Functionality is the foundation of quality. Ensure that your offering functions flawlessly and effectively delivers on its promises.

4. Embrace Simplicity: Strive for simplicity in design. Complexity can lead to confusion,

while simplicity enhances usability and aesthetics.

5. Incorporate Feedback: Seek feedback from potential users early in the design phase. Incorporate their insights to refine and enhance your offering.

6. Think Beyond Conventions: Challenge conventional thinking and explore innovative approaches. Don't be afraid to break the mold and introduce fresh concepts.

7. Future-Proof Design: Anticipate future trends and technologies. Design with adaptability in mind to ensure your offering remains relevant as the landscape evolves.

8. Balance Aesthetics and Function: Aesthetics should complement functionality. A visually appealing design enhances the user experience and communicates quality.

9. Iterative Process: Design is an iterative process. Continuously test, refine, and iterate on your design to achieve the highest level of quality and innovation.

10. Cross-Disciplinary Collaboration: Invite collaboration from experts across different disciplines. Diverse perspectives can lead to breakthrough ideas and insights.

11. Sustainable Design: Consider the environmental impact of your design choices. Sustainable practices not only

reflect responsibility but also resonate with conscious consumers.

12. Evoke Emotion: Design has the power to evoke emotions. Craft your design to create a positive emotional connection with users.

Designing for quality and innovation isn't just about aesthetics; it's about creating an experience that engages, excites, and leaves a lasting impression. Your design should reflect a deep commitment to excellence and a drive to exceed expectations. As you embark on the journey of design, remember that you're not just creating a visual or functional piece; you're crafting a representation of your brand's values, dedication, and aspirations. With each design element, color choice, and interaction, you're not just creating a product or service; you're weaving a narrative of quality, innovation, and a promise of an extraordinary experience that resonates with your audience.

Leveraging Technology for Competitive Advantage

In the dynamic landscape of business, leveraging technology for competitive advantage is the engine that propels your brand ahead of the competition. It's the strategic fusion of innovation and digital tools that allows you to not only keep pace but also lead the race. Just as a navigator uses cutting-edge tools to chart uncharted waters, entrepreneurs must harness technology to navigate the complexities of the modern marketplace, streamline operations, and deliver unparalleled value to their customers.

1. Identify Pain Points: Start by identifying pain points in your processes that

technology can address. Look for areas where automation, efficiency, or improved communication can make a difference.

2. Embrace Automation: Automate repetitive tasks to free up time and resources. Automation enhances productivity and reduces the risk of errors.

3. Data-Driven Insights: Utilize data analytics to gain insights into customer behavior, market trends, and performance metrics. Informed decisions are the cornerstone of competitive advantage.

4. Seamless Customer Experience: Leverage technology to create a seamless and personalized customer journey. From online shopping to post-purchase interactions,

technology enhances the customer experience.

5. Innovation and R&D: Invest in research and development to stay at the forefront of technological innovation. Innovate with an eye on future trends and advancements.

6. E-Commerce and Online Presence: Establish a robust online presence, including e-commerce capabilities. The ability to reach a global audience and conduct transactions online is a significant advantage.

7. Digital Marketing: Utilize digital marketing strategies to reach and engage your target audience. Leverage social media,

content marketing, and paid advertising to boost visibility.

8. Cloud Computing: Embrace cloud technology to enhance collaboration, data storage, and accessibility. Cloud computing offers flexibility and scalability.

9. AI and Machine Learning: Implement AI and machine learning to automate tasks, personalize experiences, and make predictive recommendations.

10. Customer Relationship Management (CRM): Utilize CRM systems to manage customer interactions, track sales leads, and enhance customer relationships.

11. Cybersecurity: Protect your digital assets and customer data through robust cybersecurity measures. Security is a critical aspect of maintaining trust.

12. Continuous Learning: Stay updated on technological advancements in your industry. Continuous learning ensures you're leveraging the latest tools and techniques.

Leveraging technology for competitive advantage is not just about adopting the latest trends; it's about using tools strategically to enhance your brand's value proposition. Your goal is to create efficiencies, improve customer experiences, and position your brand as a leader in your industry. As you navigate the digital landscape, remember that you're not just implementing technology; you're sculpting your brand's future. With each technological integration, optimization, and innovation, you're not just leveraging tools; you're steering your business toward a future of innovation, growth, and a competitive edge that sets you apart.

Strategic Marketing and Branding

In the vibrant tapestry of business, strategic marketing and branding are the threads that weave a compelling narrative around your offerings, captivating audiences and etching your brand into their hearts and minds. It's the art of aligning your business goals with creative storytelling and consistent visuals, creating a symphony that resonates with your target audience. Just as a conductor orchestrates each note to create a harmonious melody, entrepreneurs must strategically craft their marketing and branding to amplify their message and leave an indelible mark.

1. Define Your Brand: Start by clearly defining your brand's identity, values, and mission. Your branding should reflect who you are and what you stand for.

2. Understand Your Audience: Thoroughly understand your target audience—their preferences, needs, and behaviors. Tailor your marketing to resonate with them.

3. Develop a Unique Voice: Craft a distinct and authentic brand voice that resonates with your audience. Your tone and messaging should be consistent across all channels.

4. Create a Visual Identity: Design a cohesive visual identity that includes your logo, colors, fonts, and imagery. Visual

consistency fosters recognition and builds trust.

5. Craft Compelling Stories: Storytelling is a powerful tool. Weave narratives that emotionally connect with your audience, allowing them to see themselves in your brand's journey.

6. Content Strategy: Develop a content strategy that provides value to your audience. Create informative, entertaining, and relevant content across various platforms.

7. Multi-Channel Approach: Reach your audience through multiple channels such as social media, email marketing, SEO, and

paid advertising. Each channel serves a unique purpose.

8. Personalization: Utilize data to personalize your marketing efforts. Tailor messages and recommendations based on customer preferences and behaviors.

9. Consistency is Key: Maintain consistency in your branding and messaging across all touchpoints. Consistency builds recognition and trust.

10. Monitor and Adapt: Continuously monitor the effectiveness of your marketing efforts. Be ready to adapt strategies based on data and feedback.

11. Engage and Interact: Engage with your audience through social media, comments, and direct interactions. Build a community around your brand.

12. Measure ROI: Track the return on investment (ROI) of your marketing campaigns. Understand what strategies are driving results and adjust accordingly.

Strategic marketing and branding are not just about aesthetics; they're about creating a holistic experience that resonates with customers and builds brand loyalty. Your goal is to tell a story that goes beyond products and services, conveying the essence of your brand and the value it brings to your customers' lives. As you navigate the realms of marketing and branding, remember that you're not just crafting messages or visuals; you're creating an emotional connection, an identity, and a promise that endures. With each campaign you launch, each story you share, and each interaction you have, you're not just promoting your business; you're shaping perceptions, building relationships, and crafting a legacy of authenticity, innovation, and resonance.

Effective Brand Development and Positioning

In the ever-evolving landscape of business, effective brand development and positioning are the cornerstones that shape how your brand is perceived in the minds of your audience. It's the intentional process of crafting a unique identity, voice, and value proposition that resonates deeply and distinguishes your brand from competitors. Just as an architect carefully plans the layout of a building, entrepreneurs must meticulously plan and execute their brand development and positioning to create a foundation of authenticity and resonance.

1. Define Your Brand Identity: Start by defining your brand's core values, mission,

and personality. These elements form the foundation of your identity.

2. Understand Your Audience: Thoroughly research and understand your target audience's needs, preferences, and behaviors. Your brand should align with their aspirations.

3. Craft a Unique Value Proposition: Clearly articulate the unique value your brand brings to customers. Highlight what sets you apart from competitors.

4. Establish Brand Voice and Tone: Develop a consistent brand voice and tone that aligns with your brand's personality. Whether it's friendly, professional, or witty, consistency is key.

5. Create Visual Consistency: Design a visual identity that includes logo, colors, typography, and imagery. Consistency across visuals creates a cohesive brand image.

6. Tell Your Story: Craft a compelling brand story that communicates your journey, values, and aspirations. Storytelling humanizes your brand and engages emotions.

7. Research Competitors: Understand how your competitors position themselves. Identify gaps and opportunities to differentiate your brand.

8. Focus on Customer Benefits: Position your brand based on the benefits customers receive from choosing your products or services. Address the "what's in it for me" aspect.

9. Choose Relevant Channels: Select the communication channels that align with your target audience's preferences. Your brand should be where your audience is.

10. Consistency Across Touchpoints: Maintain brand consistency across all touchpoints, from social media to customer service. Consistency builds trust.

11. Adapt to Market Trends: Monitor market trends and customer preferences. Be

prepared to adapt your brand positioning to remain relevant.

12. Build Emotional Connection: Effective brand positioning creates an emotional connection. Align your brand with values and aspirations that resonate with your audience.

Effective brand development and positioning are more than just surface-level exercises; they shape the essence of your brand and the perception customers hold. Your goal is to create a brand that resonates deeply, establishes trust, and becomes a part of your audience's lives. As you embark on the journey of brand development and positioning, remember that you're not just creating a logo or tagline; you're crafting an identity, a promise, and an experience that extends beyond products and services. With each element you design, each story you tell, and each connection you forge, you're not just building a brand; you're shaping perceptions, fostering loyalty, and leaving an indelible mark on the hearts and minds of your audience.

Multi-Channel Marketing Strategies

In the dynamic landscape of business, multi-channel marketing strategies are the versatile tools that enable you to connect with your audience wherever they are, fostering engagement and driving results. It's the art of strategically using various platforms and channels to convey a consistent message and meet customers at every touchpoint of their journey. Just as a conductor orchestrates a symphony, entrepreneurs must harmonize their marketing efforts across different channels to create a resonant and holistic customer experience.

1. Understand Your Audience: Start by deeply understanding your target audience. Where do they spend their time? What platforms do they prefer? Tailor your strategy accordingly.

2. Omni-Channel Approach: Adopt an omni-channel approach where your messaging and branding remain consistent across all channels, whether it's social media, email, website, or in-store.

3. Diversify Your Channels: Utilize a mix of channels such as social media, email marketing, content marketing, search engines, influencer collaborations, and offline events.

4. Personalize Communication: Leverage customer data to personalize your messages for each channel. Tailored communication enhances engagement.

5. Content Repurposing: Adapt your content to fit the nuances of each platform. Repurpose content while ensuring it aligns with the channel's format and audience.

6. Integration is Key: Ensure seamless integration between your channels. For instance, include social media links in your email campaigns and website.

7. Cross-Promotion: Cross-promote your channels to create a cohesive presence. Encourage social media followers to subscribe to your emails and vice versa.

8. Timing Matters: Timing plays a crucial role. Schedule your messages to align with the peak activity times of each channel.

9. Monitor Analytics: Regularly monitor analytics for each channel to gauge performance. Understand what's working and optimize your strategies accordingly.

10. A/B Testing: Experiment with different approaches and messages. A/B testing helps you identify what resonates best with your audience.

11. Customer Journey Mapping: Map out your customer's journey and identify touchpoints where different channels can

add value and guide them through the funnel.

12. Adapt to Platform Changes: Stay updated with platform algorithms and trends. Platforms evolve, and your strategy should evolve with them.

Multi-channel marketing strategies are about more than just having a presence on various platforms; they're about creating a seamless and engaging experience that meets your audience where they are. Your goal is to create a journey that feels cohesive and valuable, whether a customer interacts with your brand on social media, through email, or on your website. As you navigate the realm of multi-channel marketing, remember that you're not just spreading your message thin; you're crafting a symphony of touchpoints that harmonize to create a lasting impression. With each post, email, and interaction, you're not just reaching your audience; you're building relationships, fostering engagement, and crafting a holistic narrative that resonates across channels.

Sales Mastery and Customer Engagement

In the dynamic realm of business, achieving sales mastery and fostering customer engagement are the twin engines that drive growth and sustain success. It's the art of not just closing deals, but also building meaningful relationships that transform customers into loyal advocates. Just as a maestro leads an orchestra with precision, entrepreneurs must orchestrate their sales efforts and customer interactions with finesse to create a symphony of value that resonates deeply with their audience.

1. Understand Customer Needs: Begin by deeply understanding your customers' needs

and pain points. Tailor your sales approach to address these concerns effectively.

2. Build Trust: Trust is the cornerstone of sales and engagement. Consistently deliver on promises to build trust with your customers.

3. Active Listening: Practice active listening during sales conversations. Understand your customers' challenges before offering solutions.

4. Customized Solutions: Offer solutions that are tailored to each customer's unique needs. Personalized offerings demonstrate your commitment to their success.

5. Communication Skills: Hone your communication skills. Clearly convey the value of your product or service and how it addresses the customer's specific challenges.

6. Relationship Building: Focus on building relationships, not just closing sales. Genuine connections lead to long-term loyalty.

7. Follow-Up: Consistently follow up with customers after the sale. This shows you care about their satisfaction and are invested in their success.

8. Provide Value: Offer value beyond the transaction. Share resources, insights, and tips that are relevant to your customers' needs.

9. Empathy: Practice empathy in your interactions. Understand the emotions and motivations behind your customers' decisions.

10. Consistent Branding: Ensure that your brand's messaging and values are consistently reflected in all customer interactions, from sales calls to customer service.

11. Anticipate Needs: Proactively anticipate your customers' future needs and offer solutions that align with their evolving challenges.

12. Continuous Learning: Stay updated on industry trends and best practices in sales

and customer engagement. Continuously refine your skills.

Sales mastery and customer engagement are about more than just transactions; they're about building a foundation of trust, adding value, and creating a lasting impact. Your goal is to guide customers through a journey that not only meets their immediate needs but also elevates their experience.

As you navigate the paths of sales and engagement, remember that you're not just making sales; you're forming partnerships, nurturing loyalty, and crafting a narrative of value that resonates with your customers. With each interaction, each solution offered, and each connection made, you're not just driving revenue; you're orchestrating a symphony of relationships, satisfaction, and success.

Persuasive Selling Techniques

In the realm of business, persuasive selling techniques are the tools that empower you to influence decisions, build rapport, and guide customers toward making beneficial choices. It's the art of presenting your offerings in a way that resonates with your audience's needs, desires, and aspirations. Just as a skilled storyteller captivates their audience with words, entrepreneurs must craft their sales approach with finesse to create a compelling narrative that leads to action.

1. Build Rapport: Establish a genuine connection with your customers. Building rapport creates a foundation of trust and receptivity.

2. Active Listening: Listen attentively to your customers. Understand their challenges and goals before presenting your solution.

3. Highlight Benefits: Focus on the benefits and outcomes your product or service provides. Help customers envision the positive impact on their lives.

4. Use Social Proof: Share success stories, testimonials, and case studies to showcase how others have benefited from your offering.

5. Address Objections: Anticipate objections and address them proactively. This shows

you understand the customer's concerns and are prepared to address them.

6. Create Urgency: Highlight time-sensitive opportunities to encourage prompt decision-making. Limited-time offers or exclusive deals can create a sense of urgency.

7. Offer Customization: Tailor your pitch to align with the customer's specific needs. Demonstrating customization shows your dedication to their success.

8. Demonstrate Value: Quantify the value your offering provides. Show how the benefits outweigh the cost.

9. Storytelling: Use storytelling to paint a vivid picture of how your product or service solves problems and enhances lives.

10. Use the "FOMO" Effect: Capitalize on the fear of missing out by highlighting exclusive features or limited availability.

11. Provide Solutions: Position your offering as a solution to a specific problem the customer is facing. The more relevant it is, the more persuasive your pitch becomes.

12. Focus on Emotion: Appeal to emotions in your pitch. Connect with your customers' aspirations, fears, and desires to make a compelling case.

Persuasive selling techniques go beyond mere transactions; they're about guiding customers toward decisions that benefit both parties. Your goal is to create a conversation that resonates, informs, and motivates action. As you navigate the world of persuasive selling, remember that you're not just making a pitch; you're crafting an experience, building trust, and igniting the desire for positive change. With each interaction, each solution presented, and each connection made, you're not just selling a product; you're creating a narrative of empowerment, value, and transformation that speaks directly to your audience's needs.

Building Lasting Customer Relationships

In the heart of business, building lasting customer relationships is the foundation that nurtures loyalty, advocacy, and sustainable success. It's the art of not just making transactions, but fostering connections that endure beyond individual purchases. Just as a gardener tends to a flourishing garden, entrepreneurs must nurture and cultivate their customer relationships with care to create a thriving ecosystem of trust, satisfaction, and mutual benefit.

1. Personalized Interactions: Treat each customer as an individual. Remember their

preferences, purchase history, and specific needs.

2. Consistent Communication: Maintain open and consistent communication with your customers. Keep them informed about new offerings, updates, and special deals.

3. Exceptional Customer Service: Provide exceptional customer service that goes above and beyond expectations. Address issues promptly and professionally.

4. Act on Feedback: Listen to customer feedback and act upon it. Show that their opinions matter and that you're committed to improving their experience.

5. Reward Loyalty: Implement a loyalty program to reward repeat customers. Offering discounts, exclusive access, or personalized perks shows your appreciation.

6. Value-Added Content: Share valuable content that educates, entertains, or solves problems for your customers. This positions you as a helpful resource.

7. Regular Check-Ins: Periodically check in with your customers to see how they're doing and if there's anything they need.

8. Surprise and Delight: Surprise your customers with unexpected gestures, like personalized thank-you notes or unexpected discounts.

9. Community Engagement: Create a sense of community around your brand. Encourage customers to share their experiences and interact with each other.

10. Transparency: Be transparent about your products, services, and business practices. Building trust requires honesty.

11. Personal Connection: When possible, establish a personal connection with your customers. Share stories, experiences, and insights that resonate.

12. Long-Term Value: Focus on the long-term value of the relationship rather than short-term gains. Prioritize mutual benefit and ongoing partnership.

Building lasting customer relationships is not a one-time effort; it's a continuous commitment to nurturing connections and delivering value. Your goal is to create an environment where customers feel valued, understood, and eager to engage with your brand. As you navigate the path of building customer relationships, remember that you're not just creating transactions; you're fostering trust, loyalty, and a narrative of partnership. With each interaction, each gesture of appreciation, and each solution provided, you're not just building customer relationships; you're cultivating a legacy of satisfaction, mutual growth, and a bond that stands the test of time.

Scaling Up for Rapid Growth

In the dynamic landscape of business, scaling up for rapid growth is the strategic blueprint that propels your brand from a budding venture to a powerhouse of success. It's the art of expanding operations, increasing revenue, and managing increased demand while maintaining quality and customer satisfaction. Just as an architect designs a building to accommodate growth, entrepreneurs must architect their strategies for scalability to create a sturdy foundation for sustained success.

1. Robust Infrastructure: Build a solid foundation that can withstand increased

demands. This includes technology, operations, and resources.

2. Scalable Processes: Streamline and optimize processes to handle larger volumes without sacrificing quality.

3. Talent Acquisition: As you grow, hire talented individuals who can contribute to your expansion. Surround yourself with a skilled team.

4. Financial Planning: Plan for financial requirements during expansion. Access to capital may be necessary to support growth.

5. Customer-Centric Approach: Maintain focus on customer satisfaction. As you grow,

ensure that your customers continue to receive top-notch service.

6. Technology Integration: Leverage technology to support your growth. Automation and digital tools can enhance efficiency.

7. Market Analysis: Conduct thorough market analysis to identify opportunities and areas of growth potential.

8. Strategic Partnerships: Forge strategic partnerships that can help accelerate your growth. Collaborations can provide access to new markets and resources.

9. Brand Consistency: Ensure your brand's identity and messaging remain consistent as you expand. Brand recognition is vital.

10. Scalable Marketing: Develop marketing strategies that can reach a larger audience without compromising message clarity.

11. Risk Management: Identify potential risks associated with rapid growth and have contingency plans in place.

12. Customer Feedback: Continuously gather and act upon customer feedback. This helps you refine your offerings and stay aligned with customer needs.

Scaling up for rapid growth requires a blend of innovation, planning, and agility. Your goal is not just to expand but to do so in a way that maintains the essence of your brand and enhances customer value. As you navigate the path of scaling up, remember that you're not just expanding your operations; you're building a legacy of success, adaptability, and sustained impact. With each strategic decision, each resource allocation, and each new milestone achieved, you're not just scaling up; you're shaping a narrative of growth, resilience, and a commitment to excellence.

Operational Efficiency and Process Streamlining

In the realm of business, operational efficiency and process streamlining are the engines that drive productivity, reduce waste, and elevate the overall performance of your organization. It's the art of optimizing workflows, eliminating bottlenecks, and maximizing resources to achieve more with less. Just as a conductor harmonizes the various sections of an orchestra, entrepreneurs must orchestrate their operations and processes with precision to create a symphony of efficiency and effectiveness.

1. Process Mapping: Start by mapping out your existing processes. Identify steps, dependencies, and areas for improvement.

2. Identify Bottlenecks: Identify points in your processes where delays and inefficiencies occur. Addressing bottlenecks can lead to significant improvements.

3. Automation: Automate repetitive tasks and manual processes wherever possible. Automation reduces errors and frees up valuable time.

4. Clear Communication: Ensure that roles, responsibilities, and expectations are clearly communicated to all team members. Avoid confusion and misunderstandings.

5. Cross-Functional Collaboration: Encourage collaboration between different departments or teams. A holistic approach can lead to streamlined processes.

6. Technology Integration: Leverage technology to enhance operations. Utilize tools for project management, communication, and data analysis.

7. Standard Operating Procedures (SOPs): Develop SOPs to establish a standardized approach for common tasks. SOPs improve consistency and efficiency.

8. Continuous Improvement: Foster a culture of continuous improvement. Regularly assess processes and seek ways to enhance them.

9. Lean Principles: Apply lean principles to eliminate waste, such as unnecessary steps, excessive inventory, and redundant processes.

10. Training and Development: Invest in training to ensure that team members have the skills and knowledge needed to perform efficiently.

11. Data-Driven Decisions: Use data and analytics to make informed decisions. Data-driven insights can reveal areas for optimization.

12. Customer-Centric Approach: Align process improvements with customer needs

and preferences. A customer-centric focus enhances satisfaction.

Operational efficiency and process streamlining are not just about cutting corners; they're about optimizing your resources to deliver value with precision. Your goal is to create a framework that maximizes productivity while maintaining quality and customer satisfaction. As you navigate the path of operational efficiency, remember that you're not just streamlining processes; you're crafting a culture of effectiveness, adaptability, and excellence.

With each optimized workflow, each eliminated inefficiency, and each enhanced process, you're not just increasing efficiency; you're composing a symphony of productivity, innovation, and a commitment to achieving more with the resources at hand.

Managing Resources and Scaling Challenges

In the dynamic landscape of business growth, managing resources and scaling challenges are the puzzles that require strategic solutions and innovative thinking. It's the art of efficiently allocating and optimizing your assets to meet increased demands while navigating the obstacles that come with expansion. Just as a navigator charts a course through uncharted waters, entrepreneurs must navigate resource allocation and scaling hurdles with foresight to ensure sustainable growth and success.

1. Resource Assessment: Begin by assessing your current resources—financial, human,

technological, and operational. Understand what you have to work with.

2. Prioritization: Prioritize your resources based on their impact on growth. Allocate resources to areas that will have the most significant positive influence.

3. Scalability Planning: Develop a clear plan for how you'll scale your operations and resources to meet increased demand.

4. Flexible Budgeting: Create a budget that allows for flexibility. Be prepared to adjust allocations based on changing needs and priorities.

5. Talent Development: Invest in developing your team's skills to ensure they can handle increased responsibilities and challenges.

6. Vendor Relationships: Cultivate strong relationships with vendors and suppliers to ensure a steady supply of necessary resources.

7. Risk Management: Identify potential risks associated with resource allocation and scaling. Have contingency plans in place to mitigate these risks.

8. Technology Adoption: Leverage technology to manage resources efficiently. Tools for project management, communication, and analytics can be invaluable.

9. Delegation: Delegate tasks and responsibilities to the appropriate team members. Empower them to take ownership and make decisions.

10. Continuous Monitoring: Regularly monitor your resource allocation and scaling efforts. Adjust strategies as needed based on real-time data and insights.

11. Cultural Alignment: Ensure that your company culture aligns with your scaling efforts. A culture of adaptability and innovation supports growth.

12. Lean Approach: Embrace lean principles to minimize waste and maximize efficiency.

Continuously seek ways to do more with less.

Managing resources and scaling challenges require a delicate balance of planning, agility, and foresight. Your goal is to achieve growth while maintaining stability and excellence. As you navigate the complexities of resource management and scaling, remember that you're not just allocating assets; you're shaping the trajectory of your business.

With each decision you make, each adjustment you implement, and each challenge you overcome, you're not just managing resources; you're orchestrating a narrative of growth, resilience, and a commitment to creating a thriving future.

Harnessing the Power of Technology

In the dynamic landscape of modern business, harnessing the power of technology is the key to unlocking innovation, efficiency, and competitive advantage. It's the art of strategically integrating digital tools and solutions to transform operations, enhance customer experiences, and drive growth. Just as an architect designs a structure with precision, entrepreneurs must architect their technology strategies with foresight to create a blueprint for success in the digital age.

1. Identify Pain Points: Start by identifying pain points and areas where technology can make a positive impact. Addressing challenges with technology solutions can lead to significant improvements.

2. Automation and Efficiency: Leverage automation to streamline repetitive tasks and processes. Automation enhances efficiency and reduces the risk of errors.

3. Data Insights: Utilize data analytics to gain insights into customer behavior, market trends, and operational performance. Informed decisions are the cornerstone of success.

4. Enhanced Customer Experience: Implement technology to create

personalized and seamless customer experiences. From AI-driven recommendations to chatbots, technology enhances engagement.

5. Cloud Computing: Embrace cloud technology for scalable and cost-effective data storage, collaboration, and accessibility.

6. E-Commerce and Online Presence: Establish a strong online presence and leverage e-commerce capabilities to reach a global audience and facilitate transactions.

7. Digital Marketing: Utilize digital marketing strategies to connect with your target audience. Social media, content

marketing, and paid advertising can amplify your reach.

8. Remote Work Capabilities: Embrace remote work technology to enable flexible work arrangements. Remote work tools enhance productivity and employee satisfaction.

9. Innovation and Research: Invest in research and development to explore emerging technologies and stay ahead of industry trends.

10. Cybersecurity Measures: Protect your digital assets and customer data with robust cybersecurity measures. Security is crucial in the digital landscape.

11. Customer Relationship Management (CRM): Implement a CRM system to manage customer interactions, track leads, and enhance relationships.

12. Continuous Learning: Stay updated on technological advancements relevant to your industry. Continuous learning ensures you're harnessing the latest tools and techniques.

Harnessing the power of technology is about more than just adopting the latest trends; it's about using digital tools strategically to enhance your brand's value proposition. Your goal is to create efficiencies, enhance experiences, and position your brand as a leader in the digital era. As you navigate the realm of technology integration, remember that you're not just implementing software; you're shaping your brand's future. With each technological innovation, each digital solution, and each strategic integration, you're not just harnessing technology; you're steering your business toward a future of innovation, growth, and a competitive edge that sets you apart.

Automation and AI for Business Acceleration

In the ever-evolving landscape of business, harnessing automation and artificial intelligence (AI) is the catalyst that propels your organization toward accelerated growth, efficiency, and innovation. It's the art of leveraging technology to automate processes, make data-driven decisions, and enhance customer experiences. Just as a conductor orchestrates a symphony, entrepreneurs must orchestrate automation and AI with precision to create a harmonious blend of streamlined operations and strategic insights that lead to unparalleled success.

1. Process Streamlining: Identify repetitive and manual tasks that can be automated to free up valuable time and resources.

2. Workflow Efficiency: Automate workflows to ensure seamless and consistent processes across departments and functions.

3. Data Analytics: Utilize AI-powered analytics to gain actionable insights from large datasets. Data-driven decisions lead to informed strategies.

4. Personalized Customer Experiences: Implement AI to analyze customer behavior and preferences, allowing you to deliver personalized experiences and recommendations.

5. Chatbots and Virtual Assistants: Deploy chatbots and virtual assistants to handle routine customer inquiries, providing immediate responses and improving engagement.

6. Predictive Analytics: Use AI to predict future trends and outcomes based on historical data. This empowers proactive decision-making.

7. Marketing Automation: Automate marketing campaigns, email sequences, and social media posts for consistent and targeted outreach.

8. Supply Chain Optimization: Employ AI to optimize inventory management, demand forecasting, and supply chain logistics.

9. Enhanced Insights: AI can uncover patterns and insights that might go unnoticed, helping you make more informed business decisions.

10. Cost Reduction: Automation and AI can reduce operational costs by eliminating manual tasks and optimizing resource allocation.

11. Innovation: AI can aid in product development and innovation by analyzing market trends and identifying unmet customer needs.

12. Continuous Learning: Stay updated on AI and automation trends. As technology evolves, new opportunities for business acceleration emerge.

Automation and AI are not just about replacing human tasks; they're about augmenting capabilities and driving strategic growth. Your goal is to create a synergy between human ingenuity and technological advancement. As you navigate the world of automation and AI, remember that you're not just implementing algorithms; you're sculpting a future of efficiency, insight, and a competitive edge that pushes boundaries. With each automated process, each AI-driven insight, and each strategic integration, you're not just accelerating business; you're conducting a symphony of innovation, optimization, and a commitment to shaping a future that's both intelligent and prosperous.

Data-Driven Decision Making

In the data-rich landscape of modern business, data-driven decision making is the compass that guides you toward informed and strategic choices. It's the art of analyzing and interpreting data to extract valuable insights, enabling you to make choices that are grounded in evidence rather than assumptions. Just as a navigator relies on charts and instruments, entrepreneurs must navigate their business journey with data-driven decision making to steer toward success with clarity and purpose.

1. Data Collection: Begin by collecting relevant data from various sources, including customer interactions, sales trends, and market research.

2. Quality Data: Ensure that the data you collect is accurate, relevant, and of high quality. Inaccurate data can lead to flawed decisions.

3. Data Analysis: Utilize tools and techniques to analyze data and uncover patterns, trends, and correlations.

4. Insights Generation: Transform raw data into actionable insights that provide a deeper understanding of your business and market dynamics.

5. Informed Strategies: Use data-driven insights to formulate strategies that are based on real-world observations and trends.

6. Risk Assessment: Identify potential risks by analyzing historical data and anticipating potential scenarios.

7. Performance Evaluation: Continuously monitor and assess the performance of your strategies using data metrics and key performance indicators (KPIs).

8. Customer Understanding: Data-driven insights help you understand your customers better, enabling you to tailor offerings to their needs.

9. Agility and Adaptability: Data-driven decision making allows you to adapt quickly to changing market conditions and customer preferences.

10. Validation and Validation: Data can validate hypotheses and test assumptions, ensuring that your decisions are supported by evidence.

11. Collaboration: Encourage cross-functional collaboration by sharing data insights across departments. This fosters a holistic understanding.

12. Continuous Learning: Stay updated on data analysis techniques and tools as data science continues to evolve.

Data-driven decision making is not about replacing intuition; it's about enhancing it with concrete evidence. Your goal is to make decisions that are grounded in reality, optimizing outcomes and minimizing risks. As you navigate the path of data-driven decision making, remember that you're not just interpreting numbers; you're uncovering insights that guide your business journey. With each data point analyzed, each trend identified, and each strategy formulated, you're not just making decisions; you're creating a narrative of precision, agility, and a commitment to steering your business toward a future that's informed and successful.

Leading for Wild Success

In the dynamic landscape of business, leading for wild success is the art of guiding your team with vision, authenticity, and innovation to achieve extraordinary outcomes. It's the skill of inspiring others, fostering a culture of creativity, and navigating challenges with resilience. Just as a captain guides a ship through tumultuous waters, entrepreneurs must lead their teams with wisdom and courage to navigate the journey toward untamed success.

1. Visionary Leadership: Set a clear and inspiring vision for your team. A compelling vision acts as a compass, guiding everyone toward a common goal.

2. Authenticity: Lead with authenticity and transparency. Your genuine leadership style fosters trust and engagement among your team.

3. Empowerment: Empower your team members to take ownership of their work and contribute their unique skills and ideas.

4. Adaptability: Navigate change and uncertainty with flexibility and adaptability. Lead by example in embracing innovation and change.

5. Effective Communication: Communicate your vision, expectations, and updates clearly and consistently to keep everyone aligned.

6. Continuous Learning: Cultivate a culture of continuous learning and growth. Encourage team members to develop new skills and knowledge.

7. Emotional Intelligence: Practice emotional intelligence by understanding and empathizing with your team's emotions, needs, and concerns.

8. Decision-Making: Make informed and timely decisions, weighing the available data, insights, and potential outcomes.

9. Collaboration: Foster a collaborative environment where team members share ideas, brainstorm, and work together toward solutions.

10. Recognition and Appreciation: Recognize and appreciate the efforts and contributions of your team members. A positive atmosphere enhances motivation.

11. Resilience: Lead by example in demonstrating resilience in the face of challenges. Your ability to bounce back influences your team's response.

12. Mentorship: Provide guidance and mentorship to help team members grow professionally and personally.

Leading for wild success is about more than just achieving results; it's about creating an environment where innovation, growth, and authenticity thrive. Your goal is not just to lead, but to inspire, guide, and shape the narrative of your team's journey. As you navigate the path of leadership, remember that you're not just directing; you're igniting potential, fostering excellence, and crafting a legacy of exceptional achievements. With each decision you make, each conversation you have, and each challenge you overcome, you're not just leading; you're creating a symphony of empowerment, vision, and a commitment to achieving wild success.

Inspirational Leadership and Team Building

In the world of business, inspirational leadership and team building are the cornerstones of fostering a motivated, cohesive, and high-performing team. It's the art of guiding individuals toward a shared vision, nurturing their growth, and cultivating a collaborative environment that thrives on synergy. Just as an artist blends colors to create a masterpiece, entrepreneurs must blend leadership and team building skills to craft a harmonious and empowered team that achieves greatness.

1. Visionary Inspiration: Cast a compelling vision that resonates with each team

member. A shared vision ignites passion and purpose.

2. Lead by Example: Set the standard by embodying the qualities you expect from your team—dedication, commitment, and enthusiasm.

3. Effective Communication: Foster open and transparent communication that encourages dialogue, understanding, and alignment.

4. Empowerment: Empower team members to take ownership of their roles, make decisions, and contribute to the team's success.

5. Strengths-Based Approach: Recognize and leverage each team member's strengths. Build roles and responsibilities around their unique talents.

6. Active Listening: Practice active listening to understand your team's needs, aspirations, and challenges. Show that you value their input.

7. Collaboration: Foster a collaborative environment where team members share ideas, collaborate on projects, and learn from one another.

8. Growth Mindset: Cultivate a growth mindset culture where challenges are seen as opportunities to learn and grow, both individually and collectively.

9. Recognition and Appreciation: Regularly acknowledge and appreciate the contributions of each team member. Celebrate wins and milestones together.

10. Continuous Learning: Encourage ongoing learning and skill development. Provide resources and opportunities for personal and professional growth.

11. Conflict Resolution: Address conflicts promptly and constructively. Help team members resolve differences and learn from disagreements.

12. Team Bonding: Organize team-building activities and events that foster camaraderie, trust, and a sense of unity.

Inspirational leadership and team building transcend traditional management; they're about creating an environment where every individual is motivated, valued, and empowered to thrive. Your goal is not just to lead a team, but to cultivate a community that is driven by purpose and achieves exceptional results.

As you navigate the journey of inspirational leadership and team building, remember that you're not just managing; you're shaping a narrative of collaboration, growth, and a commitment to reaching new heights. With each motivational message, each collaborative effort, and each shared success, you're not just building a team; you're composing a symphony of aspiration, camaraderie, and a legacy of inspired achievement.

Adapting to Change and Navigating Uncertainty

In the ever-evolving landscape of business, adapting to change and navigating uncertainty are the compasses that guide you through uncharted territories. It's the art of embracing flexibility, resilience, and innovation to thrive in the face of challenges and unpredictability. Just as a seasoned traveler adjusts their route to reach their destination, entrepreneurs must adjust their strategies with agility to navigate uncertainty and seize new opportunities.

1. Embrace Agility: Foster a culture of agility where you're prepared to adjust strategies quickly in response to changing circumstances.

2. Positive Mindset: Cultivate a positive mindset that sees change as an opportunity for growth and innovation, rather than a threat.

3. Scenario Planning: Prepare for different scenarios by considering various possible outcomes and having strategies in place for each.

4. Open Communication: Keep your team informed about changes and uncertainties. Transparent communication builds trust and reduces anxiety.

5. Continuous Learning: Encourage ongoing learning to equip your team with the skills

and knowledge needed to adapt to new situations.

6. Innovation: Embrace innovation as a way to find creative solutions to unexpected challenges and capitalize on new opportunities.

7. Flexibility: Be open to shifting directions, reallocating resources, and trying new approaches as circumstances change.

8. Risk Management: Identify and assess potential risks associated with uncertain situations. Develop plans to mitigate these risks.

9. Resilience: Build resilience within your team by helping them develop coping

strategies and mental fortitude to handle uncertainty.

10. Customer-Centric Focus: Keep the customer at the center of your decisions. Their needs and preferences guide your strategies.

11. Collaboration: Collaborate with your team to brainstorm solutions and navigate challenges together. Diverse perspectives can lead to innovative ideas.

12. Long-Term Vision: Maintain a long-term vision while adapting to short-term changes. Ensure that changes align with your ultimate goals.

Adapting to change and navigating uncertainty is not just about surviving; it's about thriving in a dynamic environment. Your goal is not just to weather storms, but to harness them as opportunities for growth and transformation. As you navigate the path of uncertainty, remember that you're not just reacting; you're shaping a narrative of resilience, agility, and a commitment to carving your own path forward. With each pivot, each decision made, and each challenge overcome, you're not just adapting to change; you're composing a symphony of adaptability, innovation, and a legacy of triumphant navigation through the unknown.

Managing Finances and Sustainability

In the intricate landscape of business, managing finances and sustainability are the twin pillars that support long-term success and responsible growth. It's the art of effectively allocating resources, maintaining financial health, and ensuring that your business practices are aligned with environmental and ethical considerations. Just as a skilled architect designs a structure for durability, entrepreneurs must design financial strategies that ensure the sustainability of their business and its impact on the world.

1. Budgeting: Develop a comprehensive budget that outlines income, expenses, and

financial goals. Regularly review and adjust the budget as needed.

2. Cash Flow Management: Monitor and manage cash flow to ensure that funds are available to cover expenses, investments, and growth initiatives.

3. Strategic Investments: Make informed decisions about where to allocate resources for maximum impact on growth and sustainability.

4. Debt Management: If using debt, manage it responsibly. Prioritize paying down high-interest debt and avoid excessive borrowing.

5. Profitability Analysis: Regularly assess the profitability of your products, services, and business segments. Focus on areas that generate the most value.

6. Sustainability Strategy: Develop a sustainability strategy that encompasses environmental, social, and governance (ESG) considerations.

7. Ethical Practices: Conduct business with a commitment to ethical practices. Transparency and ethical behavior foster trust with customers and stakeholders.

8. Diversification: Diversify revenue streams and investments to reduce risk and enhance financial stability.

9. Cost Management: Identify areas where costs can be reduced without compromising quality. Efficient cost management improves profitability.

10. Long-Term Planning: Create a long-term financial plan that includes goals for growth, expansion, and sustainability over the years.

11. Green Initiatives: Implement eco-friendly practices, such as reducing waste, conserving energy, and using sustainable materials.

12. Stakeholder Engagement: Engage with stakeholders—customers, employees, investors, and communities—to understand their expectations and incorporate their perspectives into your financial strategies.

Managing finances and sustainability is not just about short-term gains; it's about building a resilient and responsible business that stands the test of time. Your goal is to create financial stability while also considering the impact of your business on the environment and society. As you navigate the realm of financial management and sustainability, remember that you're not just crunching numbers; you're shaping the financial foundation of a business that contributes positively to the world. With each financial decision, each sustainability initiative, and each responsible practice implemented, you're not just managing finances; you're composing a symphony of stability, responsibility, and a legacy of financial health that echoes through time.

Financial Planning and Resource Allocation

In the intricate landscape of business, financial planning and resource allocation are the blueprints that guide you toward prudent decision-making, growth, and sustainability. It's the art of crafting strategies to effectively manage your financial resources and allocate them in a way that maximizes value and supports your business objectives. Just as an architect plans every detail of a structure, entrepreneurs must meticulously plan their finances and resource allocation to create a solid foundation for success.

1. Goal Setting: Clearly define your short-term and long-term financial goals.

Your goals guide your financial planning and resource allocation efforts.

2. Budget Creation: Develop a comprehensive budget that outlines your projected income and expenses. A well-structured budget is the backbone of financial planning.

3. Cash Flow Management: Monitor your cash flow regularly to ensure that you have enough liquidity to cover expenses, investments, and growth initiatives.

4. Prioritization: Identify key projects, investments, and expenditures that align with your business strategy. Prioritize allocation to areas with the highest potential return.

5. Risk Assessment: Evaluate potential risks and uncertainties that could impact your financial stability. Develop contingency plans to mitigate these risks.

6. Strategic Investments: Make strategic decisions about where to allocate funds, considering growth opportunities, market trends, and risk factors.

7. Resource Optimization: Optimize the allocation of human resources, technology, and operational assets to enhance efficiency and effectiveness.

8. Cost Control: Implement cost-cutting measures where feasible without

compromising the quality of products or services.

9. Long-Term Vision: Create a financial plan that extends beyond the immediate future. Consider how today's decisions impact your business's sustainability and growth over time.

10. ROI Analysis: Conduct return on investment (ROI) analysis to assess the potential returns of various projects or initiatives before allocating resources.

11. Continuous Monitoring: Regularly review your financial performance against your plan. Adjust your strategies as necessary based on new information or changing circumstances.

12. Flexibility: Remain flexible in your financial planning and resource allocation to adapt to unexpected changes or opportunities that arise.

Financial planning and resource allocation are not just about managing money; they're about crafting a roadmap to reach your business's full potential. Your goal is to create a resilient financial structure that supports your growth ambitions while ensuring stability. As you navigate the realm of financial planning and resource allocation, remember that you're not just making calculations; you're shaping the financial destiny of your business. With each allocation decision, each budget adjustment, and each strategic investment, you're not just managing resources; you're composing a symphony of prudence, growth, and a legacy of financial wisdom that resonates through your business's journey.

Ensuring Long-Term Business Viability

In the ever-evolving landscape of business, ensuring long-term viability is the compass that guides you toward sustained success, adaptability, and growth. It's the art of making strategic decisions, fostering resilience, and cultivating a culture of innovation that positions your business to thrive for years to come. Just as a navigator charts a course to reach distant shores, entrepreneurs must chart a course of actions that secure the future of their business and its enduring impact.

1. Strategic Vision: Develop a clear and forward-thinking vision for your business that guides your decisions and actions.

2. Adaptability: Foster a culture of adaptability that empowers your team to navigate change and embrace new opportunities.

3. Innovation: Continuously seek ways to innovate and evolve your products, services, and processes to meet changing customer needs.

4. Risk Management: Identify and assess risks that could threaten your business's viability. Develop strategies to mitigate these risks.

5. Customer-Centric Focus: Keep your customers at the center of your business

decisions. Understand their evolving preferences and adapt accordingly.

6. Financial Health: Maintain strong financial practices, including budgeting, cost control, and diversification of revenue streams.

7. Talent Development: Invest in the growth and development of your team members. A skilled and motivated workforce enhances long-term viability.

8. Market Research: Stay informed about market trends, competitors, and emerging technologies that could impact your industry.

9. Sustainable Practices: Adopt sustainable business practices that consider environmental, social, and governance factors.

10. Continuous Learning: Encourage a culture of continuous learning and improvement at all levels of your organization.

11. Collaboration: Collaborate with partners, stakeholders, and industry peers to stay connected and tap into collective wisdom.

12. Long-Term Planning: Create comprehensive long-term plans that outline your goals, strategies, and milestones over several years.

Ensuring long-term business viability is not just about survival; it's about thriving in an ever-changing environment. Your goal is not just to endure; it's to shape a legacy of resilience, impact, and lasting success. As you navigate the path of business viability, remember that you're not just making decisions; you're shaping the future trajectory of your business. With each strategic move, each adaptive measure, and each innovative initiative, you're not just ensuring viability; you're composing a symphony of longevity, relevance, and a commitment to creating a business that withstands the test of time.

Overcoming Setbacks and Challenges

In the ever-evolving landscape of business, ensuring long-term viability is the compass that guides you toward sustained success, adaptability, and growth. It's the art of making strategic decisions, fostering resilience, and cultivating a culture of innovation that positions your business to thrive for years to come. Just as a navigator charts a course to reach distant shores, entrepreneurs must chart a course of actions that secure the future of their business and its enduring impact.

1. Strategic Vision: Develop a clear and forward-thinking vision for your business that guides your decisions and actions.

2. Adaptability: Foster a culture of adaptability that empowers your team to navigate change and embrace new opportunities.

3. Innovation: Continuously seek ways to innovate and evolve your products, services, and processes to meet changing customer needs.

4. Risk Management: Identify and assess risks that could threaten your business's viability. Develop strategies to mitigate these risks.

5. Customer-Centric Focus: Keep your customers at the center of your business

decisions. Understand their evolving preferences and adapt accordingly.

6. Financial Health: Maintain strong financial practices, including budgeting, cost control, and diversification of revenue streams.

7. Talent Development: Invest in the growth and development of your team members. A skilled and motivated workforce enhances long-term viability.

8. Market Research: Stay informed about market trends, competitors, and emerging technologies that could impact your industry.

9. Sustainable Practices: Adopt sustainable business practices that consider environmental, social, and governance factors.

10. Continuous Learning: Encourage a culture of continuous learning and improvement at all levels of your organization.

11. Collaboration: Collaborate with partners, stakeholders, and industry peers to stay connected and tap into collective wisdom.

12. Long-Term Planning: Create comprehensive long-term plans that outline your goals, strategies, and milestones over several years.

Ensuring long-term business viability is not just about survival; it's about thriving in an ever-changing environment. Your goal is not just to endure; it's to shape a legacy of resilience, impact, and lasting success. As you navigate the path of business viability, remember that you're not just making decisions; you're shaping the future trajectory of your business. With each strategic move, each adaptive measure, and each innovative initiative, you're not just ensuring viability; you're composing a symphony of longevity, relevance, and a commitment to creating a business that withstands the test of time.

Resilience in the Face of Adversity

In the unpredictable journey of business, resilience in the face of adversity is the armor that fortifies you to overcome challenges, setbacks, and uncertainties. It's the art of bouncing back from adversity with strength, determination, and adaptability, even when the road ahead is rugged and uncertain. Just as a mountain stands tall against harsh weather, entrepreneurs must stand firm with resilience to weather storms and emerge stronger on the other side.

1. Positive Mindset: Cultivate a positive and growth-oriented mindset that sees challenges as opportunities for learning and improvement.

2. Adaptability: Embrace change and remain adaptable to shifting circumstances. Resilience thrives in environments of flexibility.

3. Problem-Solving: Approach challenges with a solutions-focused mindset. Break down problems into manageable parts and work toward solutions.

4. Resourcefulness: Utilize your resources creatively to find alternative solutions and navigate obstacles.

5. Emotional Regulation: Develop emotional intelligence to manage stress, frustration, and uncertainty in a healthy and constructive manner.

6. Learn from Failure: View failures as stepping stones to success. Extract lessons from setbacks and use them to refine your approach.

7. Support Network: Surround yourself with a support network of mentors, colleagues, and friends who can provide guidance and encouragement.

8. Long-Term Perspective: Keep a long-term perspective even when facing short-term challenges. Remember your ultimate goals and the bigger picture.

9. Self-Care: Prioritize self-care and well-being. A resilient leader is one who is physically and mentally strong.

10. Continuous Learning: Embrace a mindset of continuous learning and growth. Acquiring new skills and knowledge enhances your resilience.

11. Communication: Keep lines of communication open with your team, stakeholders, and partners. Transparency builds trust during challenging times.

12. Celebrate Progress: Recognize and celebrate even small victories and progress made amidst adversity. Positive reinforcement boosts morale.

Resilience in the face of adversity is not just about survival; it's about thriving despite challenges. Your goal is not just to endure; it's to emerge stronger, wiser, and more capable of handling whatever comes your way. As you navigate the journey of resilience, remember that you're not just weathering storms; you're shaping a narrative of strength, perseverance, and a commitment to rising above obstacles. With each challenge conquered, each setback overcome, and each display of resilience, you're not just demonstrating strength; you're composing a symphony of endurance, growth, and a legacy of unwavering determination.

Learning from Failures and Bouncing Back

In the dynamic realm of business, learning from failures and bouncing back is the art of transforming setbacks into stepping stones, and setbacks into comebacks. It's the skill of extracting valuable lessons from disappointments, using them to refine your strategies, and emerging stronger, wiser, and more determined. Just as a phoenix rises from its own ashes, entrepreneurs must rise from failures with resilience and renewed vigor, turning adversity into an opportunity for growth.

1. Self-Reflection: Take time to reflect on the factors that led to the failure. Analyze your decisions and actions objectively.

2. Embrace Growth Mindset: Adopt a growth mindset that views failures as opportunities to learn and improve, rather than as definitive defeats.

3. Extract Lessons: Identify the specific lessons learned from the failure. How can you apply these insights to future endeavors?

4. Adapt and Adjust: Use the insights gained to make necessary adjustments to your strategies, processes, and approaches.

5. Seek Feedback: Reach out to mentors, peers, and team members for constructive feedback. External perspectives can provide valuable insights.

6. Reframe Challenges: Reframe failures as temporary setbacks rather than permanent roadblocks. Maintain a positive perspective.

7. Persistence: Channel your determination to bounce back and overcome challenges. Persistence is key to regaining momentum.

8. Goal Reevaluation: Reevaluate your goals and objectives in light of the failure. Are they still relevant, or do they require adjustment?

9. Communication: Communicate transparently with your team, stakeholders, and customers about the lessons learned and your plans moving forward.

10. Incremental Progress: Break down your comeback into small, achievable steps. Celebrate each milestone on the path to recovery.

11. Accountability: Take ownership of the failure while also acknowledging the collective responsibility of the team.

12. Resilience Cultivation: Cultivate resilience within yourself and your team. Emphasize the importance of bouncing back and moving forward.

Learning from failures and bouncing back is not just about recovering; it's about flourishing in the face of adversity. Your goal is not just to overcome challenges; it's to use setbacks as catalysts for innovation and progress. As you navigate the journey of learning from failures, remember that you're not just encountering obstacles; you're shaping a narrative of tenacity, adaptability, and a commitment to rising stronger. With each setback analyzed, each lesson internalized, and each comeback achieved, you're not just bouncing back; you're composing a symphony of resilience, transformation, and a legacy of unwavering determination.

Conclusion

In the intricate tapestry of business, the journey to rapid and wild success is a symphony composed of strategic planning, resilience, innovation, and unwavering commitment. As we conclude this comprehensive guide, we've explored a myriad of topics that form the foundation for mastering success in the dynamic world of business.

From understanding the need for rapid and wild success to harnessing the power of technology, from strategic marketing to persuasive selling techniques, every chapter has contributed to the harmonious orchestration of a thriving enterprise.

Remember that success is not a destination; it's a continuous pursuit. Just as a conductor guides an orchestra through intricate compositions, you, as an entrepreneur, orchestrate the elements of your business to create a resonating success story. Whether you're navigating uncertainties, adapting to change, or learning from failures, each note you play contributes to the melody of your journey.

Your journey to rapid and wild success is not merely a quest for financial gain; it's an opportunity to make a lasting impact on your industry, your community, and the world. It's about embracing challenges with resilience, pursuing growth with intention, and leading with authenticity. It's a commitment to innovation, sustainability, and creating value that resonates far beyond the balance sheet.

As you take the insights, strategies, and inspirations from this guide, remember that you're not just embarking on a business venture; you're composing a symphony of transformation, innovation, and excellence. With each strategic decision, each challenge overcome, and each milestone achieved, you're not just pursuing success; you're crafting a legacy of rapid and wild success that echoes through time.

Here's to your journey of excellence, to your pursuit of wild success, and to the symphony of impact that you're creating in the world of business. Your potential is boundless, and your journey is just beginning. Embrace it with passion, courage, and the knowledge that you have the tools to master rapid and wild success in every endeavor you undertake.

Embracing Your Path to Rapid and Wild Success

In the vibrant landscape of business, embracing your path to rapid and wild success is a journey filled with challenges, triumphs, and endless possibilities. It's the art of embracing your unique strengths, pursuing innovation, and navigating uncharted waters with determination and resilience. Just as a trailblazer forges a path through the wilderness, entrepreneurs like you must forge your own path to unprecedented success.

1. Self-Discovery: Embrace your strengths, passions, and talents. Self-awareness is the foundation upon which your journey is built.

2. Vision Clarity: Craft a clear and compelling vision for your business. Your vision is the guiding star that illuminates your path.

3. Unwavering Passion: Fuel your journey with unwavering passion and commitment. Passion ignites your drive to overcome challenges.

4. Bold Innovation: Dare to innovate and challenge conventions. Embrace the courage to explore new ideas and approaches.

5. Resilient Mindset: Develop a mindset of resilience that thrives in the face of adversity. Challenges are opportunities for growth.

6. Lifelong Learning: Commit to continuous learning and growth. Stay curious and open to new knowledge and experiences.

7. Embrace Change: Embrace change as a constant companion on your journey. Adaptability is key to staying relevant and impactful.

8. Strategic Risks: Take calculated risks that align with your vision. Bold decisions often lead to remarkable breakthroughs.

9. Customer Focus: Put your customers at the center of everything you do. Their satisfaction fuels your success.

10. Collaborative Spirit: Embrace collaboration and partnerships. Working together amplifies your impact and expands your horizons.

11. Impactful Leadership: Lead with authenticity, empathy, and a commitment to empowering your team and stakeholders.

12. Reflect and Adjust: Regularly reflect on your progress and adjust your strategies as needed. Flexibility drives continuous improvement.

As you embrace your path to rapid and wild success, remember that this journey is uniquely yours. You're not following a predetermined map; you're creating your own path—one that's characterized by your aspirations, your choices, and your determination. With each step you take, each challenge you overcome, and each success you achieve, you're not just embracing your journey; you're composing a symphony of purpose, growth, and an indelible mark on the world of business.

Your potential is limitless, and your journey is a canvas awaiting your masterpiece. Embrace it with unwavering belief in your abilities and the knowledge that you have the capacity to shape your destiny. As you move forward on your path to rapid and wild success, let your passion guide you, your resilience fuel you, and your vision inspire you. Your journey is remarkable, and the symphony you're creating will resonate for generations to come.

Continuing the Journey of Business Excellence

In the ever-evolving landscape of business, the journey of excellence is a perpetual expedition that beckons with new challenges, opportunities, and horizons. It's the pursuit of continuous growth, innovation, and impact that fuels your mission to stand at the forefront of your industry. Just as an explorer embarks on an endless adventure, entrepreneurs like you embark on an endless journey of business excellence.

1. Relentless Innovation: Embrace a culture of innovation that propels you to explore new ideas, technologies, and solutions.

2. Evolving Strategies: Continuously refine your strategies to adapt to changing market dynamics and emerging trends.

3. Empowered Team: Empower your team to contribute their unique talents and ideas, fostering a collaborative environment.

4. Customer-Centricity: Remain attuned to customer needs, preferences, and feedback. Your success is rooted in their satisfaction.

5. Ethical Leadership: Lead with integrity, transparency, and ethical practices that inspire trust and loyalty.

6. Sustainable Impact: Embed sustainability in your practices, creating a positive impact on both your business and the world.

7. Lifelong Learning: Commit to lifelong learning and personal growth, expanding your knowledge and skillset.

8. Adaptability: Embrace change as a constant companion, and demonstrate agility in navigating new challenges.

9. Global Perspective: Explore opportunities beyond borders, tapping into global markets and cross-cultural collaborations.

10. Legacy Building: Envision the legacy you want to leave behind. Your journey of excellence contributes to a lasting impact.

11. Industry Leadership: Strive to lead your industry through thought leadership, innovation, and best practices.

12. Celebration of Milestones: Celebrate each milestone and achievement, recognizing the collective effort that propels your journey.

The journey of business excellence is not bound by a destination; it's a voyage fueled by your vision, your perseverance, and your unyielding commitment to growth. With each decision you make, each challenge you overcome, and each innovation you introduce, you're not just continuing a journey; you're composing a symphony of progress, leadership, and a legacy of unparalleled excellence.

As you embark on this ongoing expedition, embrace it with unwavering enthusiasm, humility, and the knowledge that your journey holds the potential to redefine industries, uplift communities, and inspire future generations. With each step forward, each strategic move, and each moment of reflection, you're not just continuing the journey; you're crafting a masterpiece of excellence that resonates far beyond the confines of time.